Pra
SHIFTFORW

D0826969

"The tone and style were very engaging and easy to follow. Love how you intertwined real, lived experiences to illustrate your points. Very timely and relevant."

—VALERIE LOVE
Senior VP Human Resources
North America, Coca-Cola Company

"This book is AMAZING. As I sat and read it I immediately recognized that I was guilty of 'blurring the lines' of diversity and inclusion. The examples given to explain the differences in each word were spot-on and funny. This book is thought-provoking for me as a person who truly wants to create a workplace culture of diversity and inclusion. By the time I finished reading the pages, I had developed my personal thought on inclusion, which is 'Inclusion is how we use our collective life experiences as humans to create a place where we all can be our best selves.'"

—ANDRADA CUNNING
Chief of Staff, Water Management Division
City of Atlanta

SHIFTFORWARD
NOW!

SHIFTFORWARD NOW!

A STRATEGY THAT MAKES INCLUSION SECOND NATURE

CHERRIE DAVIS

MOUNTAIN ARBOR
PRESS
Alpharetta, GA

ISBN: 978-1-63183-948-1 - Paperback
eISBN: 978-1-63183-949-8 - ePub
eISBN: 978-1-63183-950-4 - mobi

Printed in the United States of America   1 0 2 2 2 0

♾This paper meets the requirements of ANSI/NISO Z39.48-1992 (Permanence of Paper)

All who have encouraged me to trust my voice and thought

All who have gifted me their valuable time

All who have challenged my perspective

All who believed in me

All who love humanity and want the best for it

CONTENTS

FOREWORD

The current social and racial challenges are, unfortunately, not new. What is new is the level and depth of the conversations that are happening. While a genuine desire for change drives many of these conversations, there is confusion about where to begin and the meaning of diversity and inclusion (D&I). For many, having these discussions, there is an assumption these words are interchangeable, and one always accompanies the other—but they do not. Like peanut butter and jelly, separately, each ingredient is pretty good, but together . . . well, it can be something great.

As a senior human resources professional for multiple Fortune 500 companies, understanding what diversity and inclusion mean and the importance of these issues has always been clear to me. When you view D&I as a typical but challenging business issue, like any other business issue, you understand *"a purposeful approach with key metrics"* is the only way to achieve progress that will be sustainable. As an HR professional, I have observed time and time again the focus and metrics are hiring diverse candidates. However, the absence of understanding the culture *and* support necessary to integrate those individuals into the business's everyday workings comprehensively almost always results in a cycle of turnover.

Cherrie maps out a very practical approach to address this challenge. She brings her personal and professional experiences with the goal of simplifying a profoundly complex issue. This book will help you understand the differences between the two and the incredible benefits of having both diversity and inclusion as the goals for any organization's talent strategy. Most importantly, this book provides a road map for a journey that continues to evolve.

As you begin this work, this book offers specific exercises that help you plan your journey. Brené Brown has a saying: "We know that the way to move information from your head to your heart is through your hands."

Use this book as your travel guide. There will be many twists and turns, but like any trip worth taking, you will experience a few detours and meet interesting people who will make this a trip worth taking.

—Coretha Rushing

INTRODUCTION

CAUTION: This is meant to be taken personally.

You have finally met all of your diversity and inclusion targets. Since the last report you were able to demonstrate there was significant increase in diversities at every level of the organization. Your staff reflects adequate representation of the communities you have offices in. Your managers and directors have a cross-representation on their diversity of thought. You have a healthy pipeline of high potential leaders who represent different ethnicities and sexual preferences. Heck, your board just announced the new CEO is a Southeast Asian woman who happens to also be a lesbian. You think with all this diversity, your culture would be the best one in the industry, but it is not. Having a diverse group of people is not the complete makeup of a premier culture; it never has been enough, and it never will be enough.

At the end of the day, we all want a culture that brings out the best in us. Identifying how to get there effectively can be hard to nail down. My goal with this book is to help you leverage inclusion to construct the cultures you crave, by creating a chain reaction that starts with your mind and ends with our actions. You will learn how to envision a world where inclusion is second nature to everything you do. To help your vision of that world come into focus, I will show you how to shift your perceptions to develop habits that promote and sustain inclusion in your workplace and communities. When people started to recognize and define inclusion in earlier years as another human resource competency, it was either lumped into an abbreviated version of diversity or it was defined as nothing more than a static visual object for people's eyes to rest on, like a photograph or piece of sculptured art. To effectively explore inclusion, I quickly realized the best way to show the distinct difference between inclusion and diversity was to answer nine specific questions.

This book is meant to answer all nine questions in

an interactive way. I understand that this approach may not be for everyone, but if it shifts one person or one organization's conversation or approach on inclusion, then I did what I set out to do. As you move through the pages in Part 1, you will gain clarity and solutions to questions such as, "What is inclusion?" "Why is it overlooked?" "Does it really matter?" Then you will move into Part 2, where you will discover how your brain dictates your inclusive behavior, what are assumptions, biases, and how people categorize each other, and how fear factors into our inclusive behavior. Part 3 lays out how each player's roles, responsibilities, and expectations are relied upon for inclusion to truly be effective.

Throughout this book, stories are used of my experiences and engagements with others as a tool to illustrate situations and behaviors. Who knows—you may be able to see yourself or someone you know. You're encouraged to take time to reflect on the questions asked, then grab your favorite pen or pencil to write down your responses (yes, in the book—after all, it is yours). The curated exercises will pull double duty for you. First, you learn how your brain is the catalyst in how you discuss and approach inclusion. Second, the exercises are designed to help you gauge where you are with inclusion today and what your specific needs are to become more inclusive. Finally, there are these things called shift points that will drive home the key takeaways and how to let inclusion construct the culture we all crave!

WHY ME

My life's journey has taught me many things along the way. I realized, when it came to inclusion, I made the leap that inclusion is synonymous with diversity. As long as there is a diverse group of people in my surroundings, at home or in the workplace, I was winning in the inclusion game. That's just not true. It's FAKE news—inclusion and diversity are not the same! I now understand inclusion is what brings life to our differences; it conjures up visions of energy, activity, and interaction among people of different backgrounds, different genders, different ages, and different cultures.

Where did I get my earlier perspective? My background, as eclectic as it is, revealed that is not the case at all. What my background actually provided me with was an unwavering acceptance of people's differences at any workplace or community I am a part of. It never defined inclusion.

Growing up in New York City during the '70s and '80s, the oldest of two girls, was pretty exciting. I preferred toys that had wheels on them, like my bike or child-sized motorcycle with the big wheels on the back over plastic dolls that that were in no way a reflection of me. I read the *New York Times* newspaper, listened to National Public Radio news station, thought learning words from the dictionary was fun, and prided myself on memorizing commercials like they were lines to be delivered in a Broadway play. Our household had two moms: a Southern African American beauty with long, wavy hair, brown freckles, and fair skin; the other was an Irish American Catholic whose blond hair was cut short with shaggy bangs that accentuated her piercing blue eyes. Not exactly your typical family makeup. My childhood gifted me with this piece of knowledge: people come in different sizes, different races, and have different sets of values and beliefs. In short, it gave me real-life experiences with what a world looks like when there is diversity, but it did not prepare me to understand how inclusion moves diversity from rest and brings it to life. Just like that, I reimagined Newton's second law and its relation to inclusion and diversity.

Diversity and inclusion articulate Newton's second law in its purest form—an object at rest tends to stay at rest unless acted upon by an outside force. When we think about this in people terms, the outside force for diversity is inclusion. Diversity is static until the outside force of action is applied. The outside force is inclusion. My interpretation of Newton's second law looks like this: a diverse group of people at rest tend to stay at rest unless they are given the opportunity to be included. Which makes me believe the real engine behind diversity is the action of inclusion.

Even as a young adult, when I spent twenty-eight years serving in the military, I took inclusion for granted. Again, I thought it was all about having a variety of people with different skills. When I switched gears and moved my career into the non-profit and corporate structures as a senior leader and executive, I still looked at inclusion as that stationary piece of art. As long as there were differences in people, all was good and the inclusion box had a healthy check mark.

So, what made me shift? It was when I developed an increased curiosity about how this world could become better, how workplaces could do more than just prosper, how communities could do more than just coexist. I wondered what it would take for them to actually thrive. That's when I thought, *WE can get there once we change our conversation about inclusion.*

One of the best ways to change conversations and transform approaches to inclusion is to glean life lessons. We all have lived experiences that write the narratives to our everyday existence. This book reveals the lived experiences between me and various people I've encountered along the way. These experiences are supported by powerful points and techniques to help you successfully implement inclusion into your everyday life, making it second nature.

Changing conversations and transforming approaches to inclusion gives you the opportunity to see firsthand how inclusion is and always will be the greatest action any one of us can do for humanity. I believe individuals do amazing things on a daily basis. How people accomplish amazing things collectively can sometimes be a hit or miss. We do not always leverage or value other people's talents, perspectives, or contributions. But we can by changing our conversation and approach on inclusion. Get ready, reset, and get your SHIFTFORWARD.

PART 1

LET'S GET CLARITY

CHAPTER 1

WHAT DO YOU THINK INCLUSION IS?

> *You are not a powerless speck of dust drifting around in the wind . . . We are, each of us, like beautiful snowflakes—unique, and born for a specific reason and purpose.*

Elisabeth Kübler-Ross
Psychiatrist and Journalist

H ave you ever come across a word that sticks in the back of your mind and continues to gnaw at you until you have learned all you can about it? For me, that word happens to be inclusion. Wanting to understand this concept from different perspectives, I asked several people how they would define inclusion. What surprised me most was the definition of inclusion changed based on who provided it.

If you ask a community organizer, they would tell you inclusion means that all people, regardless of their abilities, disabilities, or healthcare needs, have the right to be respected and appreciated as valuable members of their communities. Participation in recreational activities in neighborhood settings can mean inclusion as well. If you ask an educator, they would say it means the difference in diverse students learning side by side in the same classroom. They enjoy field trips in after-school activities together. They participate in student government together. They would also add that inclusive education values diversity in the unique contributions each student brings to the classroom. Now, if you ask someone in the work environment, they would say diversity and inclusion is a company's mission. These words are often reflected in strategy statements and business practices to support a diverse workplace. Diversity and inclusion can be leveraged to achieve a competitive business advantage. The top diversity and inclusion priority is the recruitment of diverse employees. As you can see, each person's perspective renders a different definition.

The big revelation was not in the definitions; I anticipated that. The revelation was how people categorized inclusion as if it were one and the same as diversity. While factors like gender, ethnicity, sexual orientation, worldview, background, religion, age, and profession all play a part in shaping their answers, they all seemed to fall into the trap of blurring the line between inclusion and diversity. That's when I knew there was some unpacking to do between these two words. It's important not to blur the line and think inclusion and diversity are the same; they really are not. You will hear me reinforce this point throughout this book. When we blur the lines, we miss the chance to identify and appreciate the differences of each other, and how our unique qualities can create more powerful results. Here is one way to see the differences between diversity and inclusion. Diversity is when you have people who reflect different ages, ethnicities, cultures, ways of thinking, genders, faiths, and sexual orientations. Inclusion is inviting all of those diverse people to contribute their various thoughts and talents to a workplace or community. Here is a way to portray the distinction between the two words: inclusion and diversity are as distinctive as two artists.

IT'S IMPORTANT NOT TO BLUR THE LINE AND THINK INCLUSION AND DIVERSITY ARE THE SAME.

Let's look at the art styles of Picasso and Georges Seurat as a way to keep diversity and inclusion distinct in our minds. Imagine diversity as Picasso's

Women of Algiers painting, where unique shapes and colors are placed side by side while remaining distinct from each other. Picasso's art style allows you the opportunity to appreciate the uniqueness of each shape and color coexisting on one surface, without altering their original forms or colors. On the other hand, inclusion is like Seurat's famous painting *A Sunday Afternoon on the Island of La Grande Jatte*. This painting takes on a whole new meaning of seeing something new each time you see it. When you stand right next to the canvas and look at it real close, you can see Seurat painted individual dots and various colors to create the shapes on the canvas. When you step back several feet, you are able to appreciate how the individual dots morph into a cohesive picture. What a treat for the eyes! Seurat's painting effectively projects the action and science of inclusion. In this painting, you see how the different dots work together by using light to create the shading and contours of the big picture. I was truly in awe the first time I saw it. No matter how far away I am from a Picasso, it's always going to look the same. The shapes don't change, the colors don't change, and the painting doesn't visually change. There is beauty in the uniqueness of each element, just like there is beauty in our diversity. With Seurat's art, you are treated to a new visual experience depending on where you stand while you're looking at it. Using millions of dots across a seven-foot-by-ten-foot canvas and science as his major muse for the art piece, Seurat brings to life the idea that it takes intentional thought and movement of mind and contribution of talent for inclusion to be done effectively.

After looking at the painting for what seemed to be hours, I had so many questions about Seurat's technique and his patience to deal with all those dots. Just like Seurat's artistic technique, the very idea of what inclusion really means provoked just as many, if not more, questions about inclusion. What is inclusion? What does inclusion do? Is it important? How does inclusion look? Is it required? If it is required, why? Who's responsible for inclusion? Is inclusion relational or is it a process? By this time my head was about to blow off! Questions, questions, and more questions.

Most notably, how do we inspire a change in conversation that is so sustainable that it results in inclusion becoming second nature to our lives?

Based on the definitions provided, we "know" how some people think about inclusion—and if you stopped for a moment to think back on some of your previous conversations, you might be able to even determine how others "feel" about inclusion. Both only account for part of the meaning. We are still left scratching our heads with the basic question, "What is inclusion?" In academic terms according to *Merriam-Webster*, the word inclusion is defined as "the action or state of including or of being included within a group or structure." In geological terms, the Oxford English Dictionary defines inclusion as a body or particle recognizably distinct from the substance in which it is embedded.

Now that we know what inclusion is, what does it do? It oxygenates! Inclusion breathes life into our worlds by bringing diverse people to work together so they can pool different ideas and leverage all skill levels and talents to problem solve community issues or challenges that arise in the workplace. Inclusion challenges what we know of ourselves and our environment, it forces us to create and innovate. Inclusion is the lifeline to our everyday existence reflected in the most positive light. To get there, we need to do things differently and recognize the "one of each kind" mentality does not equal inclusion. I mean, let's face it—people and organizations are generally not altruistic and generous with time or resources. We got here today because of public policy, which determined disadvantaging someone based on how they look or due to a disability was not the way to go. The whole notion of inclusion is based on compliance, not goodwill. That does not mean we have to stay in that mindset.

Good news here, this is an opportunity for us to shift to the side, where the white hats save the day and behaviorally come from a place of goodwill. Now that we have untangled the meaning and intent of diversity and inclusion, we can explore the linkage the two have when referencing programs, initiatives, or business goals. How people associate inclusion and diversity reminds me of first cousins spending the summer together.

Every June, July, and August, Lisa, my first cousin from Tuskegee, Alabama, and I were inseparable. We would wake up in the morning and rush down this dirt lane that separated her house from my grandmother's house, which is where I would stay while visiting Tuskegee. There we would talk about our plans for the day, which usually consisted of climbing over the fence to pick strawberries (even though we were not supposed to), eat them as fast as possible, and play a quick game of hide-and-seek, followed by a foot race in our Chuck Taylor high-top sneakers that ended with both of us exhausted to the point we would fall asleep on my grandmother's porch in the metal swing bench, ignoring any hot spots we felt on our legs from that hot metal. We could always be caught doing the same thing, laughing at the same stuff, and almost always completing each other's sentences. My grandmother always said, "You and Lisa are like two peas in a pod!" Our energies played off of each other, complementing one another perfectly, but we were not the same person and we were meant to do different things. Lisa and I allowed our inner geologists to shine. We always looked for ways to discover something new in each other. That's the thing to remember—inclusion and diversity are not the same; they are just two peas in a pod, complementary but different. There are several companies that understand the two-peas-in-a-pod principle.

Gap Inc. and Starbucks are two great examples of companies who effectively link inclusion and diversity together without blurring the lines. In addition to business resource groups and advisory boards designed to provide opportunities for cross-cultural learning, mentoring, and relationship building among employees, Gap Inc.'s approach to inclusion is unique. It does not target a specific diversity challenge; Gap Inc. leverages their long-standing culture of equality and inclusion as a business tool to attract top talent, advance women's representation globally, increase employee engagement and retention, and drive business results.

There are four major elements of this strategy:

1. **Diversity and Inclusion Council:** Cross-section of executives from different parts of the organization work closely with human resources and leaders to guide the company's inclusion and diversity strategy by engaging employees through grassroots activities like Employee Resource Groups (ERGs). The council's approach is "think globally, act locally," with women's strategy as an area of commonality across regions and functions.

2. **Recruitment, Talent Development, and Training:** Gap Inc. leverages the signature program ASCEND, a program devoted to developing an inclusive, diverse workforce and a pipeline of future leaders. The purpose of Gap Inc.'s deployment of the ASCEND program was to help minority leaders fulfill their potential and achieve their career goals through a process of mentorship, building opportunity, and building individual capabilities.

3. **Work Life and Flexibility:** Gap Inc. recognized work-life integration as a fundamental strategy to their employees reaching full potential and thriving personally and professionally. By providing a variety of flexible working arrangements, employees' productivity, accountability, and engagement improved and thrived. The flexible working ethos has created a culture that consistently values results rather than being seen in the office by the boss.

4. **Community and Corporate Social Responsibility:** Gap Inc.'s Personal Advancement and Career Enhancement (PACE) delivers life skills, education, and technical training to women in the garment industry. To date, over five hundred thousand women and girls participate in the PACE program.

Gap Inc. received a huge payoff for their CEO, Glenn Murphy's, investment and commitment to inclusion. From 2007 to 2015, women's representation at the vice president level increased globally over 5 percent. Women of color in the United States increased over 6 percent among all employees and over 4 percent among store managers, managers, and senior managers. Direct reports to the CEO women's representation catapulted by 44 percent, with women of color being four out of the ten. Their board of directors moved the needle to the right when women's representation increased by 26 percent.

Starbucks used the linkage of inclusion and diversity to get the company back on track after two African American men were arrested for suspicion of trespassing. The manager on duty called 911 to have the men removed. The arrest happened at a Philadelphia store location where the two men sat patiently in the café while waiting for the arrival of a third person before starting their business meeting in April 2018. The arrest of these two men was especially disturbing for Starbucks because it was in direct contrast to the company's mission statement and their expectation declaration. Their mission is to inspire and nurture the human spirit—one person, one cup, and one neighborhood at a time. To drive their mission statement even further, Starbucks created an expectation that all of their retail spaces were to be more than a place to get your cup of coffee. They wanted each of their customers to be completely immersed in the coffeehouse experience. Starbucks reiterated their philosophy on the company website by publishing this statement: "It's not unusual to see people coming to Starbucks to chat, meet up, or even work. We are a neighborhood gathering place, a part of the daily routine—and we couldn't be happier about it."

Starbucks took immediate action to help the company and communities learn and move past the unnecessary arrest of the two innocent black male patrons. In a meeting with the Philadelphia mayor, police commissioner, and other government elected officials, Starbucks' chief operating officer, Rosalind Brewer, acknowledged Starbucks and Philadelphia leaders had a lot of work ahead of them and looked forward to a positive outcome. Following that meeting, Starbucks closed all its eight thousand company-owned stores across America for one afternoon in the following month to conduct racial-bias training for about 175,000 employees.

The commitment to educate their employees was an action that underscored that the problem of unconscious bias in the workplace and throughout society can prevent inclusion even on a subliminal level. Licensed stores, like ones found in Barnes & Noble or Target, received training materials after the initial sessions were completed by the company-owned stores. Starbucks took the opportunity to hone the importance of making inclusion part of their company's DNA by making racial-bias education a part of the onboarding process for new employees. Chief executive Kevin R. Johnson said, "Closing our stores for racial bias training is just one step in a journey that requires dedication from every level of our company and partnerships in our local communities," and Roz Brewer, the chief operation officer, said, "This is just the beginning of a lot of work that we plan to do together"; "We are looking at ourselves first and saying, how can we be better, and how can we do better? and to make sure that we've got the right policies and practices around our stores." This demonstrates the importance for Starbucks' top leaders to sanction and champion getting back to their founding values of humanity and inclusion.

When looking at Gap Inc. and Starbucks, I was able to understand how and why the lines are blurred between diversity and inclusion. By taking these actions, each company ensured diversity and inclusion remained synonymous with their brand and they treated inclusion and diversity as separate entities working in synergy.

Remember those questions, "How does it look?" and "Who is responsible for it?" I must admit, the "How does it look?" question challenged me the most. I kept coming back to how the people I knew experienced inclusion. Their role was to ensure the roster reflected a variety of people, like a talent scout for a major sports team. The depth of difference can be measurable and exhaustive. We have one short person, one tall person, we have representation from each race, one male, one female, all sexual orientations are represented; the physical, cognitive, hearing, developmental, visual, and behavioral disabilities are accounted for. This list can go on and on. If the team was diversified in talent and diversified with respect to ethnicity and gender, the inclusion box was checked!

Newsflash, bringing together different people does not ensure inclusion. It never has, and it never will. Believe me, I have tried in the past and it was one of my epic failures as a leader.

SHIFT POINT
Be a Geologist!
Make inclusion
recognizable and
distinct from
diversity.

CHAPTER 2

WHY IS INCLUSION OVERLOOKED?

It's not the difference between people that's the difficulty. It's the indifference.

Anonymous

W hat I am about to share is very painful. It is a story from my junior high school days, or what some refer to as secondary education. For the sake of illustrating the point of how inclusion is sometimes experienced as a spectator sport, I'm willing to take one for the team. The memory is not painful because of my athletic ability; it has more to do with realizing, for the first time, life may not always work out the way you envision it. It also has a little to do with the fashion trends of that time. It was so darn awful, to this day I am completely mortified.

It was my first gym class in my new junior high school. All the girls from the sixth, seventh, and eighth grades went into the locker room to change into their athletic clothes. At that time everyone was required to wear a gym uniform. It was a cross between a large set of stiff underwear and a short-sleeved, blue-belted onesie. Let that image sit with you for a minute . . . a hot mess. Once changed, I walked out with the unspoiled eagerness and nerv- ousness of a sixth grader ready to play her first orga- nized game of dodgeball in her new school. All the sixth graders were paired up with either a seventh grader or eighth grader. I'm thinking the teachers in- tegrated the sixth graders with the other classes be- cause of the obvious significant gaps in our size and strengths. This was probably the best way to keep my classmates and I from getting pummeled. Normally, the approach of the younger student learns from the older, more experienced student would have been a great idea, but in this case, it was not. This idea was not even marginally good; it was horrible. In fact, it was disastrous!

I, like many of the other sixth graders, walked away after that fifty-five-minute gym class dejected and irritated. Our annoyance did not come from be- ing paired up with a classmate from senior classes. It came from not truly participating in the game. None of the older kids let the sixth graders throw the ball. Instead, we just kept shuffling our feet along the boundary line with our tiny hands stretched out from our underdeveloped arms, yelling, "Pass me the ball! Hey, I am open—pass me the ball!" Which did nothing but leave us completely frustrated. I'm sure this was some sort of initiation or prank only known to the students in the senior grades. Looking back on that day, I realized it was the first time I recognized how people and situations can give you an illusion of inclusion. Which gives context to why we were so pissed off!

Unconsciously, this is where the lines between diversity and inclusion become blurred. While we had diversity by mixing the student population together, we did not have inclusion among the diverse group. In this case, the sixth graders represented a different group among others who were upperclassmen, but the critical point was they never had the opportunity to fully participate and throw the ball! The teacher's approach was intended to give us all equal access, but that did not guarantee equality to participating in the team's victory.

When I told this story during one of my keynotes, a conference participant approached me in the lobby to share his thoughts: "I really enjoyed your key-note." He went on to say, "Being a target of initiation pranks from older kids is the reason I didn't play dodgeball in school. Why would anyone want to play dodgeball?" he asked.

I looked at him square in the eye and said, "Are you serious right now?"

After a few seconds of quick reflection, I realized this was a great moment to clear up that blurred line inclusion shares with diversity. With every bit of conviction, I replied, "It's very simple; in the sixth grade, dodgeball was one of the great equalizers for a youngster growing up in NYC." Now, I knew we were not all equal in our abilities, but we did not have to be. The game of dodgeball allowed one thing: any of us, no matter what grade we were in or what our skill level was, could have a viable chance to contribute actively to the objective, which was tag everyone out on the opposing team and secure a W (win) for the team! Believe me, no one wanted to be counted out. Let's face it, when teams are forming most of us have these thoughts circling in our heads: *Please do not pick me last, and when you pick me, let me throw the ball at least one time. I want to say I helped us win!* No one, and I do mean no one, in my class wanted to miss the chance to stare down their opponent and tag them with that red dodgeball at least once. Now is about the time you may start wondering who is responsible for ensuring inclusion is actually happening. Does the responsibility lie with others? Is it an individual responsibility? Does it matter how you show up?

The answers to these questions are simple: Yes, No, Yes. Yes, the responsibility lies with others. No, it is not an individual responsibility. Yes, the way you show up matters. We will dive deeper into responsibility when we get to Part 3. For now, let's tackle the complexities of why how we show up for inclusion is often overlooked. Try this quick exercise:

SHOW UP

Draw a circle.

Now draw the circle one more time for kicks.

Why did I ask you to draw a circle of all things? For a couple of reasons. Circles are a universal silhouette. No matter who you are or where you are from, we all understand what a circle is, and more importantly, we all know there are only two directions to draw a circle: clockwise or counterclockwise. Secondly, the way you draw a circle is linked to five things: culture, written language, geography, education, and developmental psychology. All things that are taken into consideration when people think about building inclusive cultures.

Which direction did you draw your circle in? I bet your pen traveled counterclockwise. Involuntarily, with most righthanded and about 25 percent of lefthanded people, when drawing a circle, their hand travels counterclockwise. Essentially, the habits you have developed over time, coupled with skill development, determined which direction you drew your circle. This reminds me of a quote by Samuel Johnson: "The chains of habit are too weak to be felt until they are too strong to be broken."

Johnson's quote was really amplified when I read

about Google's approach to gather data on people's habits.

Google's use of 119,000 unique circle sketches drawn by people in 148 countries. The tech giant applied "simple geometry" to data from 66 countries that submitted over 100 circles. They were able to distinguish which countries favored drawing circles clockwise and which countries favored drawing circles counterclockwise. (By the way, there is nothing simple about geometry. I had to take it twice, and I still get the heebie-jeebies just writing about it!) The numbers were telling. People who were American, Czech, Finnish, Australian, and British drew counterclockwise circles 86 percent of the time. Then, Google looked at people who were Filipino, French, and German. These groups drew their circles counterclockwise 90 percent of the time and Vietnamese drew counterclockwise circles a whopping 95 percent of the time. Japan and Taiwan were the two countries that drew the circles clockwise on a consistent basis. How cool is it that something as simple as which direction you draw a circle unconsciously conveys your uniqueness—where you come from in the world? People from North America, South America, and Western Europe write their language left to right, not a lot of circular motions in the letters. People from Asian countries write their language top to bottom and are taught to write in a particular order while making one continuous stroke. When a stroke is made out of order, there is an assumption made that that person is not educated.

Now I see why it may be a bit challenging for you to break the habit of how you draw a simple shape—it makes sense it will take practice to draw your circle in the opposite direction.

Back to the question "Why is inclusion over-looked?" It's overlooked for several reasons. One, we mistake having a diverse group of people for inclusion. Remember my sixth-grade dodgeball game. I was accounted for as a team member, but I was not included in the win; I did not have the opportunity to prove my value by contributing my piercing lefthanded underthrow that gets underestimated all the time. It is a sure bet that throw will tag someone out. Another reason inclusion is overlooked: people often execute something on autopilot or out of habit, just like the circles you drew earlier. Without much thought or effort, you either drew your circle clockwise or counterclockwise. You drew your circle the same way you have drawn it all your life (unless you were required to use a different hand for some reason); you drew your circle out of habit. There is some value in accepting the habits of others. Their differences give way to various ways of seeing or doing things. We are unique, and completing the circle in whatever task will be different, and in most circumstances, we are better off for it.

THE CHAINS OF HABIT ARE TOO WEAK TO BE FELT UNTIL THEY ARE TOO STRONG TO BE BROKEN.

Joyce Hicks, a trusted expert in diversity and inclusion, shared, "I'll go on a website and I see companies have these beautiful web value statements about inclusion that'll bring me to tears they are so eloquent. Only to find during conversation that inclusive behavior is not being actualized in their day-to-day interactions and oftentimes inclusivity does not show up at the behavioral level. So, for organizations to break these old habits, they have to at least describe what the new behavior actually looks like and continue to reinforce both their published value system and requirements for inclusive behaviors."

Changing your conversation around inclusion is the first step to fully embrace an inclusive mentality and demonstrate behavior that is consistent with your inclusive mindset. When you change your conversation around inclusion, you are better equipped to adopt a new habit. That is easier said than done—most people know from firsthand experience how hard it is to start a new habit or change an old one.

Neuroscientists discovered we create habits the more often we perform an action or behave in a certain way. Once that happens, the newly created habit gets physically hardwired into the basal ganglia area of our brain. That part of the brain is responsible for our motor control, motor learning, behaviors, decision-making, and emotions. I know this is starting to sound a little like freshman Psychology 101 class, but hang in there with me. Remember, we are trying to hardwire our brains. I'll admit, I am someone who's been challenged with changing some of my habits in the past. It was hard then, but not anymore. Once I understood what actually made up a habit, rewiring my brain and creating and changing habits became easier for me, and it will be for you too.

All habits, no matter what they are, have the same psychological pattern known as the "habit loop." The habit loop is a three-part process, starting with a trigger, also known as a cue. The trigger alerts your brain to let the behavior happen by allowing your brain to go into automatic mode. The second part of the habit loop is the routine. The routine is the action you take or your actual behavior. The third and last part of the habit loop process is the reward. The reward is your brain's happy place; it's the benefit you gain from doing the behavior. The reward also serves as the part of the pattern that reminds your brain to remember the habit loop. Take a look at the habit loop in action when we discuss oral hygiene. Let's "walk" through the habit loop process using the familiar habit of brushing your teeth when you were a child and how your oral hygiene habit has changed as an adult.

YOUR OLD HABIT using the HABIT LOOP PROCESS:

Part 1: Your Cue – Loose tooth falls out of your mouth while brushing your teeth

Part 2: Your Routine – Place tooth under your pillow when you go to bed

Part 3: Your Reward – Tooth fairy leaves money under the pillow for having good oral hygiene

Some of you may be wondering whether this is really practicing a routine. It is—it's something you learned to do and practiced over and over again throughout your childhood. Once you became an adult, however, this routine stopped. Let's face it . . . all the fun of putting the tooth under the pillow in the first place was knowing you would be monetarily rewarded for putting it there in the first place. Just ask yourself, "When was the last time someone put money under my pillow?"

To change your habit, you must first change the cue or trigger that signals your brain to shift into autopilot. Then you start your new habit by changing your procedure, your routine also known as your habit. Then, to solidify your new routine into a habit, you must identify a reward that is meaningful enough to you that you will repeat the habit each time your brain recognizes the cue or trigger.

YOUR NEW HABIT using the HABIT LOOP PROCESS:

Part 1: Your New Cue – After you finish eating

Part 2: Your New Routine – Brush and floss your teeth

Part 3: Your New Reward – Keep your own teeth longer by maintaining healthy teeth and gums

Having transparency of the three parts that make up the habit loop process gives you the freedom to perform new actions repeatedly, creating a neuronal connection and cementing your new habit in your brain's basal ganglia region (or basal nuclei).

SHIFT POINT
Pass the Ball!
Everyone deserves a shot at
tossing the ball across the line
to help secure a team win!

SHIFT POINT
Switch from Autopilot!
Move past the constraints and
leverage differences.

SHIFT POINT
Get in the Loop!
Change your routine conversation
about inclusion. Create a new habit
of making inclusion a part of your
everyday!

CHAPTER 3

DOES INCLUSION REALLY MATTER?

> *What you vividly imagine, ardently desire, sincerely believe and enthusiastically act upon must inevitably come to pass.*

Paul J. Meyer
Businessman

"I'll have a grande almond-milk white-mocha crème Frappuccino, whipped cream and caramel drizzle, to go." This is how my hairstylist, Chanel Cooper, starts her day.

I asked her, "Why not just make a cup of coffee at home?" Full transparency, I am a tea drinker . . . and I make my tea at home.

She turned around and gave me a deadpan look, like I was from another planet. I said, "What?"

She said, "That is not what I want or need!" Shrugging my shoulders, I sighed and said, "Okay, tell me, what makes this cup of coffee so damn special?"

Without hesitation she started to lay it out in the most methodical way I have ever heard a cup of coffee explained. "The size matters, so I get the grande. It's the only milk I drink; almond milk is so yummy. Love the flavor, how the white mocha brings full flavor to my coffee. Since I am not a fan of caffeine, I found crème to be a better alternative. Cold blended beverages are the best; so glad Frappuccino was invented. I just love the sweetness whipped cream adds; it is one of those things that just works. Extra sweetness works for me, so that is why the caramel drizzle is always added."

Chanel's coffee order started the wheels turning in my head about how we function in our social and work climates. The reason Starbucks gives us so many choices is because they want to be as all-encompassing as possible to everyone's particular needs. I guess if they did not offer a wide range of ingredients, people would be drinking a regular cup of black coffee. Although a standard cup of black coffee might cost less, it would surely dampen the creativity people exercise when ordering their cup of joe each day.

It should come as no surprise many people don't add the plethora of ingredients in their coffee like Chanel does, which is okay. That's the beauty of individual needs and different perspectives. We all have a free choice of how we spend our money and what values we want to promote when we do. A cup of coffee is changed when it goes from coffee with sugar to coffee with cream and sugar. That same cup of coffee is dramatically transformed when it goes from those basic three ingredients of coffee, cream, and sugar to the now more elaborate set of six ingredients: almond milk, white mocha, crème, Frappuccino, whipped cream, and caramel drizzle. The flavor profile has become more complex, giving your taste buds something new to discover with each sip. Just like the ingredients in coffee, people can be enhancements. That is the beauty of different people contributing their talents. With each new contribution, you are afforded the opportunity to experience something that has more complexity and delivers on a new perspective. That new, complex experience may not be for everyone . . . but you don't know that until you try it.

Since I did not say it before, I am saying it now. I recognize there is a powerful entitlement we all hold near and dear, and that is our personal freedom of choice. What makes the freedom of choice so powerful is the knowledge and acceptance of what you may gain and the awareness concession of what you are willing to give up with your choice. The same goes for not choosing inclusion; there are repercussions that can and will be felt if we don't make inclusion second nature in our lives. You risk losing talented people, or your brand could drop its market value. Your civic image and positioning could be damaged, causing you to no longer have the following of civic-minded consumers, which could be even more damaging than losing some economic power. I would even say you can become stagnant and lag behind in your creative capabilities to develop cutting-edge innovations. At the very least, I would encourage all of us to become aware of what we are giving up when we are not making inclusion an active part of our lives.

The movie industry understood what they were giving up and what they would gain from choosing an inclusive mindset and inclusive behavior as early as 1927. This was the year the first talking picture was released, *The Jazz Singer*, starring Al Jolson, coined as a monumental event that revolutionized the film industry forever! What solidified that moment in time was when Jolson wailed out his ad lib to the title song, "Toot Toot Tootsie" with, "Wait a minute, wait a minute. You ain't heard nothing yet!" His confident and, yes, conceited call was the sound that changed the robust silent film scene from that day forward. It showed the importance of change in an already lucrative black-and-white silent film industry—how the power of sound gave the filmmakers and moviegoers a richer experience than previously released silent films.

Imagine walking into a theater expecting the experience that comes with a silent film: actors moving across the screen with words floating in to narrate the scene. Then, all unexpectedly, you hear words come from the moving mouths of the actors for the first time. The actors on the screen come alive, almost like they were in the movie theater with you. Once the actor's voice was heard, it immediately rendered the one-dimensional experience (no sound) into a lackluster experience. Whereas the two-dimensional experience gave moviegoers exactly what the producers wanted to deliver—new perspective, complexity, and the full weight of each actor's contributed talent, such as the timbre in their voice, or the variety in their facial expressions. What is the link here? Like drawing a circle, we may be on autopilot when deciding two things: is inclusion important, and is inclusion required. Make no mistake, inclusion is indeed important; without it, we would be trapped in a never-ending silent black-and-white movie, not having the occasion to gain increased insight to the emotion and meaning of words an actor is conveying in each scene. The opportunity for the producers and directors to invite different perspectives would be lost, essentially leaving us with nothing more than a one-dimensional experience, a white canvas with black and gray hues floating across it. Boring!

Determining if inclusion is required probably falls into the bucket of it's a matter of opinion. I see it like this: just like Jolson's "Wait a minute. You ain't heard nothing yet!" was dubbed the sound that changed the film industry, inclusion is the action that can, will, and does continue to transform the way we go about our everyday existence. Inclusion is that one rallying cry that signals us to assemble on the important idea of creating a diverse ecosystem and giving it life and value by enrolling people who have diversity in the areas of cognition, background, ethnicity, gender, education, physical compositions, and faith beliefs. By doing this, we demonstrate the ability to appreciate the most powerful thing about inclusion: its artistry. This is a good time to invite you to step out of your current way of thinking about inclusion into one that exemplifies its depth and intricacies. If you would, step into inclusion's art gallery. Here, you get to reimagine inclusion the same way you would a piece of art you have seen over a hundred occasions, only this time you are viewing inclusion with an innovative perspective. When you do this, you will recognize something has shifted in the way you look at inclusion.

The shift forward in your thinking gives you a new perspective that will elevate your appreciation of inclusion's "art" by transferring inclusion from diversity's two-legged frame of acceptance and respect—

the Picasso—to a scaffold whose multiple touch-points include leveraging talent, creating harmonious existence for all, launching creativity, and fostering healthy discussions that are not afraid to challenge the status quo—like the Seurat painting discussed in chapter 1. These multiple touchpoints showcase how inclusion is defined by three things: acceptance, respect, and leveraging talent. It is the action of leveraging talent that allows us to justify the requirement of inclusion and posture ourselves to create a better world.

Diversity encourages the values of acceptance and respect. Inclusion requires us to shift our mindset so that we can change our conversation and be inspired to move further along the continuum of growth as individuals who are reinforced as strong, viable networks of people in our communities and workplaces. That capability is achieved when we leverage all talent sources and value various perspectives no matter how different they are.

Now is the time to build your new muscle memory, take the switch off autopilot. Do something radical—draw the circle in the opposite direction, clockwise for some and counterclockwise for others. Enroll, learn, and tap into talent that differs from yours. With all the efforts around inclusion, there are still curiosities: How do you really get there? Is inclusion relational or process-focused? Do you create a process to put in motion or do you rely on networks of people to implement the idea? I say don't box yourself in; why not do both!

IT IS THE ACTION OF LEVERAGING TALENT THAT ALLOWS US TO JUSTIFY THE REQUIREMENT OF INCLUSION AND POSTURE OURSELVES TO CREATE A BETTER WORLD.

It takes the combined efforts of process and relationships to get the most and best of anything or anyone. Your brain is an excellent example of something that can function relationally and be process-oriented while problem solving. Have you ever done a crossword puzzle, or played a game where you had to search for a word, or guess what a word is based on several clues? These are word games consisting of letters that form words which are placed in a grid pattern, either in a rectangular or square shape. The objective of this puzzle is to find and mark all the words hidden inside the box. Most of the time a list of the hidden words is provided. These puzzles have a theme to which all the hidden words are related, such as food, animals, or colors, and at no one time are the themes ever combined. The games are relational, which show up in the various themes for each puzzle. The games are also process-driven; in order to identify the words you find in the larger pool of letters, you must put a circle around the word. Sometimes the same letters are used in a word that is diagonal or parallel to the original word.

Just like the word search games or crossword puzzles, inclusion is relational. It embodies mindfulness and intention with the way two or more people are connected in their everyday interactions with each other. Inclusion is also process-oriented, like when leaders in the community or the workplace understand how to incorporate the variety of talent and skills to meet identified objectives. At the end of the day, we want to know if we are hitting the mark. The only way to determine that is to put into practice certain steps and measure your efforts against a framework. The Society for Human Resource Management (SHRM) created a six-step method which is widely used to create an inclusive environment:

1. Educate your community or workplace network.

2. Form an inclusion council.

3. Celebrate differences.

4. Listen to each other.

5. Hold more effective gatherings.

6. Communicate goals and measure progress.

This methodology serves as a great foundation. It sets you up for success to move along the right path to an effective inclusion mindset, but it is just a start. The outlined process has clear elements: educate, form, celebrate, listen, hold, and communicate. One might say this is a comprehensive approach, but there's one thing missing—make use of the talent.

Not using the diverse talent and perspectives to innovate for or solve your organization's challenge is like having access to an unlimited arsenal during an enemy attack. When you don't use the arsenal and only use your individual handgun, you have already lost. To claim victory, unload your full firepower. To gain and keep your competitive advantage, throw hand grenades, set up land mines, and launch long-range artillery missiles. That is where the huge payoff is! When you utilize various talents and solicit different perspectives, your people become powerful and your organization becomes the gold standard. That's when you know you're moving in the right direction. When we tap into everyone's talent, we are using our whole selves, all of the brain power, all of the arms and legs, to reach the objective. Both relational and process concepts have an active role when realizing inclusion. Relational concepts are the ability to understand where people are coming from based on their lived experiences, values, and how they see the world. When you do this, you are able to value their cognitive and physical contributions. The process concept is the activation of people's contributions. The balance of these two elements will result in measurable, effective practices that change the conversations and make inclusion second nature.

SHIFT POINT
Come to Life!
Balance relational and
process strategies for
effectiveness.

SHIFT POINT
**Check Out
the Art Gallery!**
Reimagine inclusion
with a new perspective.

PART 2

AT THE CORE

CHAPTER 4

BRAIN BEFORE BEHAVIOR

Let's dare to think some bold, new thoughts, trust life a little more, unlearn some things that we've been taught. Let's spread our wings and soar.

Anonymous

T here is a demographic of people who are blowing the doors off this whole inclusion thing. The best part of it is that they don't even know they are doing it! At one point, you and I were also part of that demographic. Who are those mystical folks? They are infants, toddlers, and preschoolers. Did you know from the time we are born to about the time we turn six, none of us has any idea that inclusion is even a thing? The phrase "to see the world through a child's eyes" has a whole new meaning. I mean, when you think about it, this was the time in our lives where we had the extraordinary power to believe anything was possible. Our world was one big science project, where our learning was driven by the unknown and our willingness to experience everything. Our imaginations had no limits and nothing was off the table. These were the days we would proudly strut around in a polka-dotted shirt and striped pants. Ah, those were the days!

When we were babies and young children, each one of us was living our best life. There was no heavy cognitive lifting over inclusion. Our brain power was fueled by being in the full mix of life in the immediate moment. Think about it—we painted together, shared our crayons, and even shared our partially chewed-up gum before all the sugar was gone (a practice I don't recommend you do now). We asked questions of each other with sincere curiosity, listened to what the other had to say, even if we did not agree—because it was the polite thing to do. The best part was when the boys and girls played with abandon by trading traditional roles with each other when taking part in different games, like doctor, teacher, or my favorite, jump rope.

Back in the Bronx, it was no big deal for me to challenge any of the boys on the block to a game of jump rope. Most of the time, all the kids crowded around to see who could jump the fastest and longest in one of our many double-dutch contests. Peter was the one boy who usually accepted the challenge first. He would jump so feverishly his mouth would fall open, exposing the wide gap between his front two teeth. Sweat saturated his striped shirt just like the one Ernie wore on *Sesame Street*. He was so serious. Peter would win the speed portion of the contest, but I had lots of stamina. I would actually put my brain into gear and think to myself, *Just keep going, you can win*, even when I was tired. I am convinced this helped me to jump the longest and beat Peter. No matter the outcome, we always had lots of fun. To be honest, I don't remember having pressure to act one way or even have role restrictions placed on any of the kids I played with. I even had a racetrack instead of a dollhouse. We were living the high life. All was good in our world—unless, of course, someone took your favorite blanket or insisted on feeding you peas, which by the way still have a high yuck factor for me! So, when did we start going through life with the hampering habit of bucketizing everything and everybody?

We started putting people into groups, what is also known as bucketizing, from the day we were born; we just did not know we were doing it. Remember, we didn't even know about inclusion; it was just how our brains naturally worked. Instead of ruling someone out because of the way they looked or what they believed in, we would rule people out because of the way they made us feel. I can recall at a very young age hating to see one of my mother's friends, Ms. Francis, come to our house. For some odd reason, she would greet me by pinching one of my cheeks between her long, thin fingers. That pinch left my face twinging with pain for what seemed to be a full minute once her fingers released my skin. After a few encounters, I moved Ms. Francis permanently into my "do not get near me" bucket of people. Again, not because of how she looked, but because of how she made me feel. Looking back, I can see how science plays a big part in how we think about, approach, and implement inclusion. In chapter 2, we touched on how the basal ganglia region of the brain develops habits and skills. Just like the well-trained competitor from *American Ninja Warrior* needs to know the makeup of the "mega wall" in order to scale it successfully, you need to understand from a neuroscience perspective what part of your brain scales the inclusion wall so that you can successfully make your communities and workplaces more inclusive.

To get a general awareness of how the brain is wired and examine its capabilities, let's take a high-level look at certain parts of the brain. The limbic brain is where the emotions are managed, and there are three parts of the brain that regulate our fight-or-flight response to danger: hypothalamus, amygdala, and hippocampus. Our neocortex is responsible for high-level thinking, problem solving, language, planning, vision, and pattern recognition; some of this functioning is on a conscious level. We are aware of what we are doing and are intentionally putting effort toward our behaviors or actions. By now, you are either reaching for your receipt so you can return this book or you are asking, "How does this have anything to do with inclusion?" I assure you, it has everything to do with inclusion.

Our brain is one of the most rigid muscles in our body. It also happens to be the primary muscle used in inclusion; it does all the heavy lifting. Sometimes, the heavy lift of thinking about something differently can feel like an impossible task because:

1. Our brains are not wired to change the conversation about inclusion without some serious intentional work on our part.

2. There are roles and responsibilities ingrained in the brain's functionality before any of our behavioral development begins.

We are going down this line of thinking so that you can understand the power and function of the brain as it relates to inclusion. Once you are able to do that, you will be better equipped to shift your behaviors and inspire others to adopt inclusion as second nature in their everyday lives.

Most of us have at least one habit that does not support inclusion as defined in this book. It could show up in what we say, how we say it, what we do, how we do it, and to whom we are directing our message or behavior to. No matter what our habits are, at one point in time we have all tried to break one of our habits, or we know someone who has tried to change one of their habits. Oftentimes it's disguised in New Year's resolutions, or something that has to be done because it will save our lives. Many times, our efforts to create, change, or break a habit are met with enthusiasm and willingness to do things differently or better, but can result in us falling short of our desired goal, leaving us discouraged, defeated, or worse, dead. What does it take to change a habit successfully? Keep in mind, success is not just acquiring or changing the habit; success is measured by your ability to sustain your new habit.

Your likelihood of success comes when you rewire your brain by identifying three things: what is your current conversation or behavior, what do you want to shift in your current conversation or behavior, and what or how would you change your conversation or behavior to support making inclusion second nature in your engagements with others. Using the Shift with Intention (SWI) process will increase your chances of successfully breaking, changing, or creating your new habit. At any given time, you have the power to focus on conversation and behavior individually, or you can choose to work on them simultaneously.

SUCCESS IS NOT JUST ACQUIRING OR CHANGING THE HABIT; SUCCESS IS MEASURED BY YOUR ABILITY TO SUSTAIN YOUR NEW HABIT.

SWI PROCESS

Identify 1–3 of your own current messages or behaviors that do not support inclusion. What needs to shift to support inclusion (i.e. tone, attitude, or action)?

CONVERSATION/BEHAVIOR NOW

1. _____

2. _____

3. _____

WHAT TO SHIFT

1. _____

2. _____

3. _____

MESSAGE/BEHAVIOR DESTINATION

1. _____

2. _____

3. _____

SHIFT POINT
Rewire Your Brain!
Create new habits with
intention to support
inclusion in every aspect
of your life.

CHAPTER 5

Our ABCs: Assumptions – Bias – Categories

> *We, as a people, we have a strong need to categorize everything. We put labels on everything and it's a totally understandable need because we are animals and we need to understand order and where to fit in.*

Armin Van Buuren
DJ and Record Producer

E veryone on this planet, to include your clergy, the nice lady down the street, and even the wise family member who "has seen it all in their lifetime," has the same die-hard habit: they assume who someone is and what their behaviors are. Believe it or not, this is one way our brain conserves energy. On any given day each one of us kicks into autopilot with no effort. We make assumptions about events or people by drawing on our past experiences to find patterns on how the world works. There is just one problem with this technique. Whenever we encounter a new situation, we tend to apply our existing patterns to them. These existing patterns then become our assumptions applied to the diverse canvas of people.

You are Indian, so you must know a lot about computers . . . here is another dumb blonde . . . young people today are so lazy, they have no work ethic. Most black men know how to rap, indigenous people either have a drinking problem or they abuse drugs, wearing a hijab signals you're a female terrorist, gay men are flamboyant and rude, women won't return to the workforce after they have children. In fairness these may not be assumptions you've made personally, and this is certainly not an exhaustive list of them. All of these statements are tough to hear. Nonetheless, they are assumptions many people have made about someone at some point.

Assumptions are even more problematic because they are not fully based on anything experiential. To be clear, assumptions are things that are accepted as true or as certain to occur without proof of it actually ever happening. Our assumptions are based on what is occurring inside of us. Think of a fancy cocktail you learned to make from an award-winning mixologist. The mixologist expertly blends your assumption cocktail with six organic ingredients: 1) firsthand observations, 2) empathies, 3) spiritual beliefs, 4) emotional temperament, 5) mental composition, and 6) personal philosophy. Let me be clear—assumption cocktails are not solely made by a mixologist; people more often than not make their own special brand of an assumption cocktail. We traverse through life, curating something no one else will ever be able to replicate. We draw from our individual emotions, desires, expectations, and beliefs to validate our assumption. If you pour additional ingredients into it, your fancy cocktail can turn into the crazy punch from your high school senior prom! Just like that crazy punch, your assumptions cause you to develop narratives or beliefs that are not necessarily grounded in truth. Our storylines and viewpoints provide the foundation for our biases, creating an environment for inclusion to be glossed over in our personal and professional lives. This is where we fall back into that "illusion of inclusion" behavior identified earlier. I call this "coloring inside the lines," when our lived experience narrows and warps our peripheral view of the larger world. Coloring inside the lines allows our assumptive habit to create alternate realities even when there is no basis of truth to them. About this time the danger alarm should be going off in your head. The more your assumptions are not supported by reality, the more likely you can create problems and misunderstandings for others and yourself. Even with good intentions, our assumptions and biases can make changing our conversation around inclusion hard.

To reset and change the conversation, it takes us being committed emotionally, cognitively, and behaviorally. A few years back, I facilitated a three-day leaders' retreat for seventeen people of a well-known company. The youngest participant was thirty-five years old and the person with a little more road under their tires was sixty-two years of age. These leaders wanted to get together to address biases within the organization and lay out a road map to help integrate inclusion into their business. Each came in with a sense of determination that was only matched by their sense of commitment to give it their all. These folks had a genuine desire to have the most eminent inclusive workforce. That initial evening before day one of the retreat, we went through the normal routine of introductions, setting up ground rules, and identifying the challenges as experienced through each participant's lens.

The group agreed to commit and honor four ground rules. Ordinarily, this is no big deal, but in the case of this group, I already knew there was going to be a problem. What raised the red flag was the language used to build out the third ground rule, "Leave all assumptions behind." I knew immediately the group would struggle with honoring this ground rule. At each turn, their assumptions and biases would work against their efforts, even when they did something as simple as eat a piece of candy. This was sure to happen because people are usually not aware of their assumptions and biases. What we often believe to be fact is really an unverified assumption.

Day one, I gave each participant a pack of original Starburst candy for their midmorning snack. Each person would rip open their candy, dump it on the table, and subconsciously begin separating them into four "invisible buckets," pink, yellow, orange, and red. It was even more interesting when I was able to score the original flavor packs of Starburst, where the red candy is replaced by the original green candy. People assumed that their packet of candy was defective because they expected a red candy and not a green one. As the day went by, candies were consumed at various times throughout the day. Most people ate one grouping of candy first before moving on to the next one. By the end of the day I would informally ask each person, "Why did you separate your Starburst that way?" The replies ranged from "I eat my favorites first" to "I like seeing the colors separated" or "I eat the one I like least first."

Day two, I gave out packets of plain M&Ms. For the record, I prefer the ones with peanuts, but participants got the plain ones in case anyone had a nut allergy. The same habits unfolded almost identically to when they had their Starburst candy. Instead of four "buckets," most of the people had six: red, orange, green, blue, yellow, and dark brown. At the end of the day, I did another informal query asking why they separated their M&Ms candy that way. The responses were surprising to me; they were so similar to their answers from the previous day when they ate the Starburst candy. People shared, "I like to eat my favorites before spending time on the other ones," "I like to see how many of each color I have," "The candies look more appealing separated," and "I eat the chocolate ones first—they are my least favorite." Your least favorite, WHAT THE WHAT? That makes no sense to me at all. Both candies have various colors in the bag, but Starburst is the only one with different flavor profiles. No matter the color of the M&M shell, there is only one flavor in the bag—and that is chocolate!

This made me think back to how our habits are formed—through repetitive action until they become ingrained and can be performed with little effort. The way each person ate their Starburst or M&Ms consistently highlighted four of the six criteria:

1. **Firsthand observations:** Organized candy into specific piles

2. **Emotional temperament:** Candy brought back memories of their childhood

3. **Mental composition:** Displayed their candies for visual stimulation

4. **Personal philosophy:** Developed a specific way they were going to consume the candy

No matter how irrational it might have seemed, people were really invested in different ways to consume their candy. They had strong convictions about the taste or perceived taste and thoughts around what order to eat the candy in. Heck, some people had even convinced themselves the M&Ms were flavored differently because the Starburst had four flavors. The whole ritual of how people ate their candy highlighted a powerful concept. Until we break our cycle of assumptions that have become habits, we will always fall short of ensuring inclusion is a continual part of our lives. People go through life creating emotional temperaments about something they do not understand even though they have observed it firsthand. When that happens, they refine it into a mental composition that helps to develop and reinforce a personal philosophy. That is dangerous. When that happens people will have a reflex or habit to not enroll the person who might have contributed to their assumptions or biases.

Some of the greatest challenges any one of us faces are breaking old habits, developing new ones, and then successfully maintaining the new habits. From firsthand experience, I know this to be true. Until recently, I, too, struggled when trying to create a new habit. What changed? My approach to habit creation changed. Remembering my habits are assumptions that are hardwired in my brain, I knew to start with the psychological aspect of habit creation. Instead of leaning on preconceived notions of people, I now take time to figure out how each person I encounter impacts me. Shifting my mindset becomes easier when I go through what I call the "H3I" process:

1. HOW: Am I receiving firsthand information about the person?

2. INFORM: What am I learning from this encounter?

3. INFLUENCE: How can this person persuade me?

4. INSPIRE: What does this person do to move me?

This mental exercise trains the mind to not fall into assumption mode. The H3I process gives you the insight to push past the desire to prematurely categorize people into your "constructed buckets." You will chip away at old mindsets and behaviors, break free, and rewire your brain to create new habits that support inclusion at home and in the workplace. Alan Alda once said, "Your assumptions are your windows to the world. Scrub them off every once in a while, or the light won't come in."

When you let "new light in," meaning you let a person in, you are more likely to recognize a person's value and provide opportunity for their value to come to life with real contribution.

ALAN ALDA ONCE SAID,
"YOUR ASSUMPTIONS ARE YOUR WINDOWS TO THE WORLD. SCRUB THEM OFF EVERY ONCE IN A WHILE, OR THE LIGHT WON'T COME IN."

SHIFT POINT
**Train Your Mind to Leave
Assumptions Behind!**
Rewire your brain to create
and maintain new habits.

CHAPTER 6

BFFs:
Big Fear Factors

You gain strength, courage, and confidence by every experience in which you really stop to look fear in the face. . . . You must do the thing which you think you cannot do.

Eleanor Roosevelt
First Lady

"If you're scared, say you're scared!" Growing up, this phrase was used to call you out on a dare. If you completed the dare, you were golden and "lived" to see another day, but if you backed out of the dare, you were called a "scaredy cat" and your fears were on full display.

Fast-forward to now. I'm a grown woman whose age is hovering just past the fifty-yard line, I am of sound mind, and I have served honorably in the Army for twenty-eight years, defending the United States of America during the Herzegovinian-Bosnian conflict, the War in Afghanistan, and the Iraq War. Clearly, I'm no pushover. I am brave and courageous in any situation . . . unless it involves a reptile. I'll give you a moment to stop laughing before I continue with this story.

On a recent trip to Mexico, I saw a three-foot white iguana strolling back into a cement retaining wall that separated the sandy beach from the walkway. When the iguana finally settled in with his head and shoulders sticking out of the wall, watching tourists go by, all I kept thinking about was how I was going to muster up the courage to walk past this thing. I was so afraid that I almost missed out on my massage because, one, I could see him, and two, I had convinced myself at any moment this reptile was going to jump out and attack me. Which was ludicrous, since meat is not part of an iguana's diet. Iguanas like plants, flowers, and tree leaves. Clearly, I wasn't in any danger, but that did not matter to me—I was scared.

A whole year goes by and my fears are realized again, only this time the reptile is very different from the iguana in Mexico. This time the reptile is a male green anole, a.k.a. a lizard, that insisted on using my patio and flower boxes for his personal tanning bed. When I first saw him, I totally freaked out, screaming at the top of my lungs for help as I made a beeline for the patio door while never turning my back. Each time after that, I still freak out. The mere sighting of this seven-inch creature, with his sharp nose, narrow head, slender body, and long skinny tail, sends shivers up my spine and paralyzes me until I come to my senses and scamper off to the safe zone, previously identified to be behind my closed patio door. I can't count how many times I have tripped and sprained my toes in my haste to ensure the lizard stays outside as I quickly slam the door behind me. It's safe to say no matter the size of the reptile, I have a HUGE fear of these things. When I think about my reaction to reptiles, this little guy garnered the same reaction as that three-foot iguana in Mexico. What is that about?

Back in chapter 4 we discussed the amygdala as being the part of the brain that causes these reactions and insecurities. Which means my brain functions like the Dropbox app used to store your documents, and in my brain's case, it is storing my fears and anxieties. My brain recalls the three-foot iguana and manages the impulsive emotion of fear and anxiety every time I see a reptile of any size.

Fear and anxiety are just like my cousin and I: two peas in a pod. They are considered to be closely related; both words convey the notion of threat or possibility of harm. Overall, fear is perceived as a reaction to a specific observable danger, and anxiety is something we develop in our heads. In short, anxiety is a perceived threat. Like when I thought that three-foot iguana would leap out of the cement wall and have me as its afternoon snack. It takes a lot of intention and hard work on my part to overcome that fear and not freak out every time I'm confronted by a reptile no matter what size it is. Here's the funny thing, I know my fear of reptiles is irrational. Tell that to my brain— maybe one day I will get a handle on it!

When fear shows up, our brain shifts into protective mode. If a person is in a situation that they perceive as harmful, whether real or imagined, a threat stimulus from the amygdala region of the brain shows as fear. Just like a surprise dinner guest who shows up at your door with a bottle of wine, fear also shows up with a hostess gift. Fear triggers the release of stress hormones, and our fight-or-flight motor functions are activated. After all this has happened, all a person wants to do is immediately remove themselves from the threatening situation.

People can similarly demonstrate fear when it

comes to inclusion. They have reasons like they did not grow up with different races, that person's values and beliefs differ from theirs, they have a negative perception of a person from another country, that person is limited because of a physical disability, or they don't understand a person's fluid identity (he/she/they/we). When this happens, the elements of combustion are primed: igniter, fuel, and oxygen. These elements can create a fire wall of flames up to 150 feet and barrel through an area as fast and as loud as a moving freight train. Fires like this burn for days, sometimes months. The thing with wildfires is the longer they burn, the harder it is to put them out. What's really dangerous— our fears and anxieties are like these wildfires. When our fears and anxieties become entrenched and are left unanswered, they turn into a monstrous, sweltering combustion that will rage through our workplaces and communities like the eight-hundred-plus wildfires that burn across California each year. This can make inclusion feel like a steep, uphill climb with limited visibility because your eyes are constantly running due to the hot, black, thick smoke. The embers and ash in the air burn your throat, prohibiting you from taking a breath. Needless to say, you are uncomfortable and things become real hard.

THE THING WITH WILDFIRES IS THE LONGER THEY BURN, THE HARDER IT IS TO PUT THEM OUT.

Take a look at the seven wildfires that have blazed through and scorched several inclusion efforts in workplaces and communities: 1) conversations are uncomfortable, 2) it is not an intuitive behavior, 3) time is not dedicated, 4) it is tied to an unspoken cause, 5) the depth is too big to tackle, 6) people can't connect the dots, and 7) people refuse to change.

On their own merits, you could easily dismiss these as seven little fires and move on to something bigger, but that would be a grave mistake. These little fires can easily grow into large wildfires. When any of these seven wildfires are left unattended, they will destroy your organization by eroding trust among your people, and when trust is compromised, cultures are damaged. That is where the real danger lies.

Wildfires are life threatening for any organization—they devour your time, drain your people, and negatively impact your financial resources. They spread fast, causing irreversible damage. To put them out, firefighters use a technique called "hotspotting." To help you wrap your mind around hotspotting, think of this technique in the same way you think of nurses using triage to prioritize patients in an emergency room. Instead of people, firefighters are "triaging" fires. Firefighters check the expansion of fires at points of more rapid spread or special threat. After the fire team gauges the wildfires, they can turn their attention to how to extinguish the fire and prevent further damage. What a great technique! You can use this technique to get rid of fears/anxieties about inclusion and reinforce trust and commitment in your communities and workplaces to move forward and thrive.

Let's clear the thick, heavy, black smoke away so we can clearly see why these "wildfires" make inclusion difficult and what "hotspotting" we can do to put them out!

WILDFIRE 1:
CONVERSATIONS ARE UNCOMFORTABLE

Our identities and sense of belonging are engrained in positive experiences and negative experiences. People find it uncomfortable to talk about their personal lives at work or with people they do not know well. The sayings "Keep your personal business at home" and "Don't let anyone see your weakness" are a way certain cultures prepare individuals to navigate social situations outside of the home. By doing this, walls are not only erected between people who are different, they are also reinforced. The way people are identified expands at a fast rate, and sometimes it is hard to know what the correct terminology is. People are scared of saying the wrong thing to the wrong person at the wrong time. This expansion of categories can be overwhelming, leaving you a bit confused on how to include them mindfully and leverage the differences effectively.

HOTSPOTTING 1:
OPEN UP

You can strike an acceptable balance between

sharing more of your personal story with others and protecting your privacy. One of the more effective ways to strike that balance is through social situational awareness. With practice, you can gain critical awareness of your surrounding environment and use that information to make decisions that lend themselves to opportunities that allow you to openly share details about yourself, resulting in better understanding of who you are, what you value, and how you can contribute to the greater whole. Words that are spoken with truth, authenticity, and openness will enable inclusive environments, allowing people to see all of you. For people to open up about themselves with true authenticity, it is important they understand the common foundations of how we see ourselves. Dr. Celia de Anca and Dr. Salvador Aragon wrote an article in *Harvard Business Review* summing up the three types of diversity that shape who we are and how we see ourselves:

> Demographic diversity is tied to our identities of origin (gender, race, sexual orientation)—characteristics that classify us at birth that we will carry

around for the rest of our lives. Experiential diversity is based on life experiences that shape our emotional universe. Affinity bonds us to people with whom we share some of our likes and dislikes, building emotional communities. Experiential diversity influences what we might call identities of growth (affinities, hobbies and abilities). Cognitive diversity makes us look for other minds to complement our thinking, what we might call identities of aspiration (how we approach problems and think about things).

These three types of identities give us a common foundation of how we see ourselves, help us to humanize our existence to each other, recognize a common bond between each of us, and create pathways for different identities to work together.

WILDFIRE 2: INCLUSION IS NOT AN INTUITIVE BEHAVIOR

I truly believe inclusion is not an intuitive behavior. Oftentimes the assumption is made when there is a diverse population represented in the workplace or in our communities that all of those people are contributing their thinking, talents, and skills. In fact, it rarely happens this way. Just because there's diversity doesn't mean everyone has been provided the opportunity to contribute. Simply put, we more often than not miss the opportunity to behave as if inclusion is intuitive because we fall prey to our programmed assumptions.

Instead, we can approach inclusion as a situation that can be remedied by pulling a group of like-minded people together who share several commonalities amongst themselves, known as affinity groups. This group would feel a sense of security and kinship because of their common threads. Or worse, you launch bias training because something goes wrong among different demographics in the workplace, like discrimination in the workplace or in the community. Then you find something needs to be done quickly to address prevent possible negative ramifications.

HOTSPOTTING 2:
MOVE PAST AFFINITY GROUPS AND BIAS TRAINING

Bias training is something that is needed but should not be used as a knee-jerk reaction to address social issues around race. Affinity groups are a healthy way for people to reconnect to others; however, they are not the best solution to address inclusion. Instead, create opportunities that empower people to intentionally incorporate one another's thoughts about what inclusion is and how they would like it to look in action. A great way to get started is to use these questions to get an initial assessment of your environment: Is there a reliance or identity preference based on one of the three identities listed above in Hotspotting 1—identity of origin (gender, race, sexual orientation), identity of growth (affinities, hobbies, and abilities), or identity of aspiration (how we approach problems and think about things)? If so, what can you do to enroll active involvement from as many identities as possible? What I have learned is people who want to be more inclusive rely on individuals to bridge the gap. We will get into that in the next chapter when we look at roles and responsibilities.

WILDFIRE 3:
TIME IS NOT DEDICATED

We just don't make time for inclusion. Or when we do, it is not enough time, which is even worse!

HOTSPOTTING 3:
DEMONSTRATE THE VALUE OF INCLUSIVENESS
Make inclusion part of the work that increases the bottom line, or that makes your community better. Carve out and commit the time needed for inclusion to become second nature in your communities and workplace. Hold everyone accountable for the failures and the accomplishments.

WILDFIRE 4:
INCLUSION IS TIED
TO AN UNSPOKEN CAUSE

Using inclusion to address race, gender, prejudiced attitudes, or social imbalance due to the historical institutions of racism will only render solutions that are frail and have no chance of sustainability. You must first be willing to address the topics that prevent inclusion from happening in the first place.

HOTSPOTTING 4:
BREAK THE SILENCE

There is no automatic pass when difficult topics come up. Ignoring them only festers insecurities, accelerates fears, and inflates anxieties. This is a bad combination. You should speak up and ask questions if you are not sure about something. Take the opportunity to peel back conversations and ask the hard questions—"why" a person may feel that way or "what" drives the person to engage in a certain way. You should even gain clarity and ask what the best word or phrase is to use when describing different groups of people. These "why" and "what" questions give each of us a look inside the window of the person's belief system. Put more trust in your authentic attempt to be inclusive than in your passiveness potential when a can of worms is opened. Do not allow fear to silence your genuine curiosity.

WILDFIRE 5:
THE DEPTH IS TOO BIG TO TACKLE

There is no way to change the way people think. It's overwhelming, and even those with lots of resources are challenged by how people feel and think about inclusiveness.

HOTSPOTTING 5:
KNOCK 'EM DOWN ONE AT A TIME

Could you imagine being able to understand the objectives of people, and to think about what's going on in someone else's head? A social cognitive skill called "theory of mind" lets us do just that. The theory of mind allows you the ability to demonstrate an understanding that others have intentions, desires, beliefs, perceptions, and emotions different from your own and it is those intentions and desires that affect people's actions and behaviors. To develop and strengthen your social cognitive skills, try working through these five applications. Heads up, this is real work here. Most of us can rationalize people are not the same, therefore they may want different things, have different beliefs. Heck, we can even understand someone may have a false belief about something. Where it becomes difficult is when people's hidden emotions cause them to act differently from what they are truly feeling. People have a hard time dealing with other people's emotions. This is why the level of difficulty increases as you work through each application:

Application 1 – The understanding that the reasons why people might want something (i.e. desires) may differ from one person to the next.

Instance 1 – Tanya eats homemade strawberry ice cream because it is her favorite flavor. Lorrain doesn't like to throw away ripened strawberries, so she is going to make a pint of strawberry ice cream.

Application 2 – The understanding that people can have different beliefs about the same thing or situation.

Instance 2 – Howard believes beestings will kill him. Cameron believes beestings are harmless.

Application 3 – The understanding that people

may not comprehend or have the knowledge that something is true, also known as hindsight bias or the "I knew it all along" phenomenon.

Instance 3 – Leslie notices it's beginning to look cloudy and gray outside. She says to herself, "I bet it's going to rain later." When it actually does rain, Leslie tells herself, "I knew it would rain when I saw the clouds moving in earlier."

Application 4 – The understanding that people can hold false beliefs about the world. A good correlation to remember—familiarity breeds belief.

Instance 4 – It takes seven years to digest swallowed chewing gum.

Application 5 – The understanding that people can have hidden emotions, or that they may act one way while feeling another way.

Instance 5 – Craig is sad his team was not recognized for their innovative efforts but puts on a smile and uses an upbeat tone of voice when conveying the news to his team.

It's fair to say inclusion is not a hundred-meter

dash. It takes a fair amount of patience, planning, and stamina, especially when it involves our brain. Over time, you will see micro shifts in thoughts and perceptions of others as you hone your social cognitive skill. Our brains are the strongest organ we have; wield it with confidence and power. Celebrate the small changes that render progressive steps and deliver wins toward inclusion becoming second nature in our behaviors!

WILDFIRE 6:
PEOPLE CAN'T CONNECT THE DOTS

People are often not sure of the practical steps that will lead to an inclusive culture. The domino effect from not executing on a plan are lost ideas, silent resignations, and stymied cultures.

HOTSPOTTING 6:
GET RID OF USING THE WORD "INITIATIVE"

Just remove it from your vocabulary entirely when discussing or working on creating an inclusive culture. The word "initiative" denotes a definitive start time but does not always have a prescribed end time.

This can be very challenging for any environment. When an initiative drags on with no destination in sight, attention fatigue creeps in. People will lose sight of the goal and there could be long-term negative impacts. Once that happens, interest and involvement fade off. People will conclude that inclusion is not worth their time or effort; it won't be an essential part of their community or company DNA.

On the flip side of the coin, let's say you are able to engage people to work toward creating a more inclusive environment, but they respond because it's a requirement, not because they have bought into the concept of inclusion. That type of engagement would likely be lackluster at best. When people engage in an uninspired way, it could feel like the office party you did not want to go to but did so out of obligation to the team. This kind of event does nothing but leave you feeling like you have wasted an hour of your life.

To prevent a culture of people feeling like they are wasting their time, develop a plan for inclusion that will actually succeed. Begin with identifying what you want your environment to be. This is the time to dream and think big and not put limits on what inclusion can look like and be for the organization. Remember, you can always scale back later.

Be the role model for inclusion. Enroll a cross-functional group of people from the three different identities discussed in Hotspotting 1: demographic diversity, experiential diversity, and cognitive diversity. When you enroll these identities, you give people from all levels of the organization the chance to take the reins and be part of the plan's successful solution.

The best way to set your path on the effective track and keep people engaged is to start simple. Decide on no more than three action items that will help achieve your outcome. Don't complicate your efforts. Be sure to apply timelines to your action items; it will help keep everyone's skin in the game. Follow up on the plan's progress, trust yourself and your people. Don't forget to gift people the chance to adjust the plan as needed. Sometimes giving people a little running room can be difficult for leaders. I get it, but keep in mind, when people decide to believe in having an inclusive environment, they will engage. In fact, they will have just as much of a desire, if not more, to see inclusion succeed, especially if their contributions are valued.

WILDFIRE 7:
PEOPLE REFUSE TO CHANGE

There is no skin in the game for some people to change.

HOTSPOTTING 7: FACE REALITY

This is where we take our rose-colored lenses, or what I call purple glasses, off. There will always be a small fraction of individuals who do not see any benefit to themselves in an inclusive culture. Some may even think it will disrupt their personal ecosystem. That is just a fact. The key is to give them a chance to get on board. If they choose not to get on the right side of history, respect them, watch them, and ensure they do no harm to others who are investors and champions of inclusion. In other words, do not allow the opposition to unduly influence the energy around you. They could adversely impact your climate and good works. Focus efforts on those who support inclusivity. After all, everyone is afforded an opinion.

SHIFT POINT
Put Out the Wildfires!
Do not allow fear and
anxiety to spread.

PART 3

IN FULL EFFECT

CHAPTER 7

WHO'S IT GONNA BE?

You have tremendous flexibility in defining both the greater good and the greater community. If you don't succeed in this, then you will continue to pull that heavy wagon up the mountain, and despite the fact that you are pulling it, it will somehow run over your own foot.

Srikumar Rao
Speaker and Author

W hen it comes to inclusion, I believe it takes the effort and commitment of everyone, no matter who they are or what they do. As stated earlier, it is the uniqueness of our contributions that allows us to thrive, be creative, and sustain peak performance. To show my perspective in a more vivid way, I want you to look through a set of lenses I have placed in front of you. One lens depicts the evolution of inclusion and its original intent to "change the workplace and change the world." The other lens brings into focus a detailed account of what inclusion looks like in a very unconventional way.

Peering through the first lens shows the emergence of inclusion starting as early as 1961 when President John F. Kennedy signed an executive order establishing affirmative action requirements for government contractors. The passing of the Civil Rights Act made it illegal for employers to discriminate on the basis of race, sex, religion, or national origin. By 1964 we saw the establishment of the US Equal Employment Opportunity Commission (EEOC). By the '70s, the Supreme Court had given the EEOC the authority to sue for discrimination, companies provided affirmative action training to prevent litigations, and Xerox took center stage when their African American employees formed seven independent alliance groups, representing the first employee resource groups (ERGs) in the workplace.

The late '80s brought attention to the landmark study, *Workforce 2000: Work and Workers for the 21st Century*. In this study, the Hudson Institute predicted a changing workforce that would be older, have more female representation, and be multicultural and racially diverse. Even though race and culture refer to people, groups, and their classifications, each word is extremely different in how people are classified. Both of these terms, race and culture, are classifications of people. "Race" is a classification of people according to their physical appearances, geographic lineage, and heritable characteristics, whereas "culture" is a classification of people according to their beliefs and values that include spirituality, religion, language, and income. Although the study was released in 1987, it had been only twenty-three years since the establishment of affirmative action. That is why the Hudson Institute's findings were such a big deal. Just like diversity and inclusion, people often did not always distinguish between race and culture; people had a tough time wrapping their minds around the whole multicultural and racially diverse concept. Even more fascinating was how the five challenges outlined in the study are the same challenges we are still talking about and grappling with today: stimulating world growth, improving productivity in service industries, reconciling the needs of women/work/family, improving the dynamism of an aging workforce, and improving worker's education skills.

When I first read the *Workforce 2000* study, I believe it was the first time I felt there was a need for inclusion to be considered a separate entity from diversity. My conviction of inclusion being defined as an action grew stronger as we moved into the '90s when the Americans with Disabilities Act was signed into law.

Sixty-three percent of major companies shifted their focus from taking positive steps to get individuals into their organizations to creating an inclusive culture that provided diversity training to improve people's awareness, attitude, knowledge, and skills. The diversity training was a great step in the right direction, but I liken it to how a new bike with only the front wheel would ride. No matter how hard you pedal, you are going nowhere fast. To improve your bike-riding experience and actually get somewhere, you have to install the rear tire. That rear tire is what puts your bike in motion. Just like the rear tire on your bike, inclusion (the rear tire) was needed to leverage the newly acquired diverse workforce (the front tire).

The evolution continues with the signing of the Family and Medical Leave Act, which afforded new parents twelve weeks of unpaid leave to care for their newborn child. Which brings us to the doorsteps of the 2000s, where the fruits of leveling the playing field show up in a variety of ways. The Lilly Ledbetter Fair Pay Act strengthened protections against pay discrimination, Ursula Burns was named the first black female CEO of a Fortune 500 company, workplaces and communities were becoming more diverse, and research revealed the business case for diversity and inclusion (D&I) and the high cost of bias. CEO activism rose when more than ninety executives spoke out against North Carolina's anti-LGBT percent diversity on their boards. Growth in Fortune 500 companies and board diversity went up from 69 to 145, equaling a 40 percent increase. By 2019, Fortune 500 companies had thirty-three female and three African American male CEOs. As you can see, there were a lot of legislative hands in the responsibility pot. Once these various bills were enacted into law, there was still no clear-cut template for responsibility and roles—and by the way, inclusion was slowly coming out from the shadows of diversity.

People were taking notice and trying to figure out inclusion's who, what, where, and how. What did people do when inclusion became a thing? To establish responsibility, most organizations passed the D&I baton over to someone who could influence and encourage people to adopt inclusive behavior; in the early stages, it was usually a midlevel leader. At first this seemed to be the way to go, but as time passed, organizations, no matter the size or industry, allowed competing requirements to quickly take hold, leaving inclusion to dissipate in the wind like a directionless goose-down feather that has escaped from your pillow. When this course did not render good results, organizations changed lanes and hired consultants trained in D&I work, usually a team of two—an African American woman and a white man—who would deliver the training. These teams pulled double duty, no pun intended. They were seen as essential to exposing different races' perspectives and they were thought to model cross-racial collaboration. This proved to be an unsustainable staffing solution for many organizations, resulting in companies identifying an internal D&I professional from the existing head count (again, usually a minority woman). The internal D&I professional held people's feet to the fire to get objectives on track and keep them moving forward.

Were there any potential roadblocks to inclusion? These initial steps were made with good intentions but unfortunately, it often turned out not to be the ideal solution. For starters, people felt as if the D&I professional was nothing more than "the super checker," the person who built the scorecard and delivered communication one-liners as needed by leaders to demonstrate they were paying attention to inclusion. Not to mention, the journey to inclusion is riddled with roadblocks, making it very difficult to get any real traction. Time, people, and dollars are usually the three roadblocks set up across a one-lane road, forcing inclusion efforts to be stalled or completely stopped. At times these roadblocks would even merge with one another, compounding their negative impacts for inclusion efforts to succeed. Here's what I mean:

> **Roadblock 1: Time** – There is never enough, especially in today's environment. When there is not enough time dedicated to inclusion goals, you won't be able to do the heavy lifting needed for brains to shift and behaviors to change.

People are compelled to choose where to focus their energy. Do you focus on what you've been hired to do, or do you spend time on something that will not be reflected in your performance review? Most people would apply their energy to what puts money in their pockets.

Roadblock 2: People – From my own accounts, having enough people with the right talent to meet stated goals continues to be the Achilles' heel of all corporate, nonprofit, and community organizations. D&I efforts are usually envisioned by some but championed by one. Rarely is it the case when everyone dedicates some level of effort to creating, delivering, and supporting inclusion so they can move them away from being programs to being a core part of the company culture.

Roadblock 3: Dollars – Then we come to dollars, arguably the most contentious of the three roadblocks. When the funds are not allocated, no amount of planning or people will get you closer to inclusion. This leaves D&I professionals to rely on their individual ability to influence their counterparts, colleagues, and leaders to do three things: carve out time on their calendar, sanction their existing team members to donate talents, and earmark a portion of their budget to keep inclusion top of mind in the organization.

Are people ready to commit to inclusion? Most of the time the answer is no. There can be no commitment to inclusive efforts until people are able to see inclusion as a competitive advantage. In a good number of cases, D&I professionals' requests are met with polite lip service and no real commitment to action. Why is that? Why do people waste time providing lip service with no real commitment to take action? I interviewed Valerie Love, the Senior VP of Human Resources North America for the Coca-Cola Company, to hear what her thoughts were. Her response was quite enlightening: "Businesses have not collected voices from all the different demographics (age groups and lifestyles) which create the competitive advantage. I don't think we do it well." She did not just base that on her current assignment with the Coca-Cola company.

Valerie also shared, "This is my fourth multinational company and none of us have done it well, but there are companies that do it really well."

Based on her response, I asked, "If a business is to do well, must it have a workforce that looks like the client(s) it serves?"

"Yes, let your workforce reflect your consumer population. If you're going to market to me in a black community and you have no black marketers, good luck with that. If you don't reflect your employee base the same way you are looking at how you market to your consumers, you've missed the boat. For example, being a black woman, I can tell you more about the black community of women than fifteen Harvard graduate white women who have read several data points all day long. The reality of the situation is it does not matter what you studied, or how many white papers you've written. I think until we make it a business priority, it's still an initiative."

This is where Valerie and I strongly agreed. The real move is from initiative, as we discussed in chapter 6, to business imperative. Valerie ended her comments with this: "The one other thing I would tell you, Cherrie, is diversity gets a lot of attention, but inclusion doesn't."

I shouted, "Bingo, you and I are on the same sheet of music!" This has been my point all along. Inclusion deserves its own landscape. Let me share with you the one time I actually saw inclusion at its best.

Take a look through the second lens. While on safari, my guide Alfred showed me firsthand how the entire animal ecosystem used their unique skills and talents to thrive in South Africa's Kruger National Park. Most interesting was recognizing the impacts the inclusive behaviors actually had on living and working together. After all, inclusion is not just for the workplace—it is for every place there is life! It took the animals of this game reserve to illuminate that. The five characters that really struck a chord with me were the cape buffalos, the terrapins, the hippos, the elephants, and the mighty bee-eaters. I warned you, this was going to be unconventional.

Each one of these characters understood how vital it was to be part of the inclusion solution. They contributed their unique skills and talents for the betterment of their fellow habitants and the overall welfare of their community. I was in total awe of each animal's ability to know their responsibility, purpose, and impact to the greater whole. The cape buffalo is considered the bulk grazer. They are responsible for converting the long grasslands into short, grassy environments that become advantageous to those with short grass–grazing habits. I called the cape buffaloes Kruger Park's iron chefs. The terrapins put their swimming prowess on full display each time they transported the variety of land frogs back and forth across the watering hole. The terrapins easily earned the Uber driver role. Hippos are dubbed the engineers of the ecosystem; using their large bodies, they create channels in the water and paths on land to redirect water, which constructs habitats and shelters for smaller creatures. The quality controllers of the ecosystem are the bee-eaters. Their diet consists mainly of poisonous insects, ensuring those pesky insects do no harm to the environment. Which brings us to my favorite character, the elephants.

I considered these gentle giants the tenured professors with many hidden talents. Elephants know about everybody and everything in the ecosystem, due to their long life-span of up to seventy years and their incomparable memory. Elephants have multiple roles. They are natural team builders; they are farmers, water managers, land developers, and interpreters. Most elephant behavior has to be learned, so they keep their offspring with them for many years. Females stay with the herd indefinitely while the males leave after maturity, which happens between their twelfth and fifteenth year. Their eating habits create gaps in vegetation, allowing new plants to grow. When the waterhole is dry, they use their tusks to dig for water and share what they find with other creatures around them. Seeds found in their dung grow new vegetation, helping the fight against climate change. The best part—elephants are known to have complex consciousnesses that are capable of strong emotions. Which means they meet and greet you where you are and rely on all of the other species to complement and complete their animal ecosystem with the greatest impact. Based on that life-changing experience on safari, the importance of changing our conversation and approach to inclusion was even more amplified.

I love how the CDC drove my point home with this quote on their official website: "Inclusion should lead to increased participation in socially expected life roles and activities—such as being a student, worker, friend, community member, patient, spouse, partner, or parent." Their quote really lends itself to the idea inclusion is not just diversity on steroids. It takes more than representation for us all to successfully make inclusivity part of our everyday. It takes major involvement!

Effective involvement could potentially be stalled if you are unable to see things in a different light. For you to be able to see things differently, your cognitive flexibility may need to be strengthened. You may need to take steps to build your capability to see things differently in midstream. A memorable demonstration of cognitive flexibility is experienced when you play the UNO card game. At the beginning of the game, everyone starts out discarding their cards matching by number. The rules can change at any point when someone starts playing by color or action. This means you will have to shift your thinking and change your mindset to realize you have shifted from playing by numbers to playing by colors or actions, which will require you to depart from your original strategy to win. Those who don't shift their mindset and fail to engage their cognitive flexibility usually miss the chance to win at UNO.

EFFECTIVE INVOLVEMENT COULD POTENTIALLY BE STALLED IF YOU ARE UNABLE TO SEE THINGS IN A DIFFERENT LIGHT.

Now let's switch back to the original question: "Who has responsibility for inclusion?" If you responded everyone is responsible, you have successfully shifted your one-dimensional thinking about "who is responsible" for inclusion to a multifaceted thought of "who are the people participating and what are they contributing?" This demonstrates you have committed to move past your cognitive rigidity to adapt to your cognitive flexibility. Make no mistake, it takes discipline to increase your cognitive flexibility, since it is determined by your temperament, social learning, and environment. Shaking up my routine and learning new things are my two favorite ways to keep my brain limber. They are relatively easy to implement and cost little to nothing to do.

Shake up your routine. To keep the mind sharp and flexible, introduce new things into your everyday. New stimuli require your brain to adapt quickly, which promotes cognitive flexibility. Change your route to and from work or to your favorite activity or a community event. Take a different side road when walking in your neighborhood. Sit down for a conversation with people who are totally different from you. These are excellent ways to get your brain to make new connections. Learning new things like a language, a new game, or even an instrument will absolutely enhance your cognitive flexibility as well.

Now that we know how to ensure our minds get and stay pliable, it's time to look at the breakout of roles needed to get inclusion around those road-blocks and on the open highway. The WE grid on the next page will help you deliver scope and clarity to everyone's role by outlining two things: WHAT each role is and the EXPECTED outcomes for each role.

WE Grid

The Role	*Expected Outcomes for the Role*
Accountable	The person who is accountable to the business (in some cases the board) or the community for success. Strategic decisions related to the project or initiative are made by this person.
Responsible	One or two people who are responsible for day-to-day execution, making sure the work gets done within project constraints and meets our standards of excellence. Tactical decisions related to the project or initiative are made by these folks.
Participant	People who allocate time and resources to support the project's delivery, but for whom the project is not a primary role or responsibility. They make decisions related to the quality of the work, but they otherwise look to the Responsible or Accountable party for direction.
Advisor	People who are consulted on various aspects, but they have no decision-making authority.
Livewires	People who demonstrate inclusive behavior in their everyday work life and in their communities.

Source: Adapted from ARPA template, a derivative of the RACI matrix. Nick Francis, Help Scout.

By understanding the roles and their deliverables, you will be able to untangle any confusion. People will be more empowered to adopt their roles effectively and increase the frequency for inclusion to be achieved and sustained as part of their everyday engagement with others.

SHIFT POINT
Remove the Roadblocks!
Ensure everyone
understands what their
role is and the expected
outcomes.

CHAPTER 8

ALL HANDS
ON DECK

I believe that, if managed well, the fourth industrial revolution can bring a new cultural renaissance, which will make us feel part of something much larger than ourselves: a true global civilization. I believe the changes that will sweep through society can provide a more inclusive, sustainable, and harmonious society. But it will not come easily.

Klaus Schwab
Founder, World Economic Forum

H ave you ever heard someone say, "There are too many cooks in the kitchen"? This is figurative speech for when there are multiple people involved with something and their participation could potentially have a negative impact on your culture's climate, the individual participants, and accomplishing targeted objectives. It also invokes what is known as the Ringelmann effect, or social loafing.

Social loafing occurs as one person expends less effort on something when working in a group compared to working by themselves. You can observe social loafing best when people are rendering applause. During applause, individual people can basically hide behind the crowd's effort. By the way, the bigger the group is, the less responsibility an individual feels is needed on their part to ensure the group's success. Try this reflective exercise.

Think about the last time you gave applause for

something or someone. Did you start clapping when the applause was already in full mode? Was your clapping a symbolic gesture with no sound made? Did you stop clapping while the rest of the audience was still applauding?

If you answered yes to any of these questions, you at some point have given in to social loafing when you did not use total effort to ensure your clapping contributed to the thunderous sound of the group's applause. Now imagine being in a group where several people do that. Their applause would come across as flat, which is worse than not clapping at all.

Social loafing shows that as group size increases, individuals believe two things: they do not have to clap as loud or as long, and there are enough people in the group to get the job done—i.e. other people's applause will be loud enough without their full participation. This can happen anytime groups require individual contributions for the organization's success.

Other variables like identifiability, personal relevance, group cohesiveness, and task interdependence also contribute to the phenomenon of social loafing. For instance, if a person does not feel critical to the company's or community's success, it becomes easy for an individual to put in less effort, or worse yet, disengage completely. Each if not all of these events could easily happen to any group of any size, especially if that group is simultaneously responsible for something as big as inclusion. Groups will continue to grapple with social loafing if steps are not taken to mitigate it.

SOCIAL LOAFING SHOWS THAT AS GROUP SIZE INCREASES, INDIVIDUALS BELIEVE TWO THINGS: THEY DO NOT HAVE TO CLAP AS LOUD OR AS LONG, AND THERE ARE ENOUGH PEOPLE IN THE GROUP TO GET THE JOB DONE.

Making use of a Functional Approach using Intentional Movement, what I call the FAIM strategy, is one of the surest ways to prevent social loafing from derailing individuals' efforts as they work in groups:

FAIM STRATEGY

1. Build meaningful buy-in.

2. Ensure each person understands their contribution is identifiable (how their efforts fit into the larger picture).

3. Make it important to everyone. Find ways for inclusion to have relevance to each person.

4. Cultivate a tight-knit team; foster a sense of responsibility for one another.

5. Make inclusion a strategic endeavor and business imperative.

6. Live and work by the creed "It takes us all to build and sustain inclusive cultures."

When you apply the FAIM's six components to your inclusion efforts, individual persons will commit their fullest energy, remain tuned in, and deliver your group's requirements.

SHIFT POINT
Deliver Thunderous Applause!
Use your total talent
to get the job done.

CHAPTER 9

ONE MORE THING

You're not obligated to win.
You're obligated to keep trying
to do the best you can every day.

Marian Wright Edelman
Civil Rights Activist

A t the core of my being, I believe inclusion matters because we say it matters. I also believe that recognizing it matters is not enough. Inclusion can only work when we want it to. For that want, that desire, to take hold we must fully commit our energies to this chain reaction. Change the conversation about inclusion so that mindset shifts and inclusive behavior becomes second nature to how we live and how we work.

Having the distinct pleasure of exchanging thoughts with thought leaders and effective practitioners continues to afford me reminders that widen my lens on best practices. During one such time, Coretha Rushing, Chair Emeritus for the Society of Human Resource Management (SHRM), shared, "You know, Cherrie, inclusion is the chance for different people who are part of the team to have an equal opportunity to succeed and/or fail."

Check, check, and double-down check! I absolutely prescribe to that line of thinking. When you fully embrace inclusion as an opportunity for your diverse group of people to utilize each other's strengths and preferences to fail or succeed, you are that much closer to creating inclusive communities and inclusive workplaces. You will be equipped to respond to the times you fail and poised to effectively identify best practices to sustain your success!

SHIFT POINT
Commit to Inclusion!
You will fail and fall, so just
get up and pick up where
you left off. With practice,
discipline, and patience, you
will excel and soar!

BIBLIOGRAPHY

Auger-Dominguez, Daisy. "Getting Over Your Fear of Talking About Diversity." *Harvard Business Review.* November 8, 2019.

Cherry, Kendra. "How the Theory of Mind Helps Us Understand Others." Very Well Mind. April 7, 2020.

Cleveland, Shelle. Telephonic interview. May 19, 2020.

Cooper, Chanel. In-person interview. April 7, 2020. Given permission to use interview content in book.

Corliss, Richard. "The First Talking Picture" from "80 Days That Changed the World." *TIME.* March 31, 2003.

Deeble, Mark, and Victoria Stone, dir. *The Elephant Queen.* Apple TV, 2019. Documentary Film.

Dishman, Lydia. "Millennials Have A Different Definition Of Diversity And Inclusion." Fast Company. May 18, 2015.

Doerr, Patsy. "Four Companies That Are Getting Diversity & Inclusion Right – And How They're Doing It." *Forbes.* November 5, 2018.

Duhigg, Charles. "Habits: How They Form And How To Break Them." Author Interviews. National Public Radio. March 5, 2012.

Explainer. "The Value of Inclusive Education." Open Society Foundations. May 2019.

Gurchiek, Kathy. "6 Steps for Building an Inclusive Workplace." SHRM.org. March 19, 2018.

Ha, Thu-Huong, and Nikhil Sonnad. "Different Strokes." Quartz. June 15, 2017.

Hampton, Debbie. "The Neuroscience of Changing Your Behavior." The Best Brain Possible. January 8, 2017.

Handratta, Venkatesh, MS, MD. Assistant Professor, Georgetown University Hospital. June 2020. Provided guidance for the neuroscience aspects of the book, Habit and Skill Theory of Mind and Cognitive Flexibility from a psychological discipline.

Harned, Brett. "How to Clear Project Confusion with a RACI Chart [Template]." Team Gantt. September 16, 2019.

Heshmat, Shahram. "Anxiety vs. Fear." *Psychology Today*. December 3, 2018.

Ibrahim, Lobna, MD. Staff Psychiatrist, DC Veterans Hospital. May 2020. Provided guidance for the neuroscience aspects of the book, Habit and Skill

Theory of Mind and Cognitive Flexibility from a psychiatric discipline.

Institute for Community Inclusion. "What We Mean When We Talk About Inclusion." University of Massachusetts Boston. Accessed August 26, 2020.

Javanbakht, Arash, and Linda Saab. "What Happens in the Brain When We Feel Fear." Smithsonianmag.com. October 27, 2017.

Johnston, William B., and Arnold E. Packer. *Workforce 2000: Work and Workers for the 21st Century.* Washington, DC: Hudson Institute, 1987.

Kravitz, D. A., and B. Martin. "Ringelmann Rediscovered: The Original Article." *Journal of Personality and Social Psychology* 50, no. 5 (May 1986).

Lanciego, José L., Natasha Luquin, and José A. Obeso. "Functional Neuroanatomy of the Basal Ganglia." *Cold Spring Harbor Perspectives in Medicine* 2, no. 12 (December 2012).

Love, Valerie. Telephonic interview. June 4, 2020. Given permission to use interview content in book.

Michel, Alexandra. "Sparking Change." Association for Psychological Science. December 23, 2019.

Mondal, Somen. "Diversity and Inclusion: A Complete Guide for HR Professionals." Ideal Blog. March 4, 2020.

National Wildfire Coordinating Group.
https://www.nwcg.gov/term/glossary.

Oppong, Thomas. "The Neuroscience of Change: How to Train Your Brain to Create Better Habits." Medium. June 2, 2018.

Polonskaia, Alina, and Mark Royal. "How the World's Most Admired Companies Drive D&I." Human Resource Executive. December 10, 2019.

Rushing, Coretha. Telephonic interview. May 12, 2020. Given permission to use interview content in book.

Starbucks Stories and News. "Starbucks to Close All Stores Nationwide for Racial-Bias Education-on May 29, April 17, 2018.

About the Author

Cherrie Davis is a recognized visionary leader and speaker who draws on more than thirty-two years of experience leading strategic human resources, change management, and coaching strategies in the defense, nonprofit, and corporate sectors. She provides a fresh perspective to her clients by merging real-world experience with proven knowledge of human resources and the real need to align with organizational goals. Cherrie keys on two things: the individual and the process. By doing so, she can relationship-build, drive positive performance, and deliver winning solutions.

Cherrie's career landed her in key assignments

worldwide to lead and influence change in Hungary, Bosnia, the North Atlantic Treaty Organization (NATO), Afghanistan, Iraq, South Korea, the Pentagon, Our Lady of the Lake, GE Lighting, and GE Capital. She culminated her military career at the Pentagon by leading the Army chief of staff's transitional strategy in three pivotal roles: chief of operations for Transition Strategic Outreach, deputy director for Transition Strategic Outreach, and employment director for the Soldier for Life program. In her civilian career, Cherrie served as the human resources director for Our Lady of the Lake, quality trainer and organizational developer for GE Financial Services (Six Sigma Team), and marketing and sales for GE Lighting. Her corporate culmination came as an executive for GE Capital as the senior integration leader.

She is the founder and president of SHIFTFORWARD, a human solutions firm, based in Atlanta, Georgia. Cherrie received her BA in communications from Black Hills State University, Spearfish, South Dakota, where she was recognized as the Distinguished Military Graduate and by Who's Who among Students in American Universities and Colleges. She earned a master's in human resources with an emphasis in international management from Webster University, St. Louis, Missouri. She holds professional certifications for Senior Professional Human Resources, Executive & Organizational Coaching, and Quality Management.

Cherrie's Speaking Topics

Leadership
Culture
Inclusion & Diversity
Communication
Military Veteran

Follow Cherrie on Social Media

- ShiftForward
- Cherrie Davis
- @ShiftForward2
- @cherrieldavis
- www.cherriedavis.com